Buff-laced Wyandotte

White-crested Black Poland

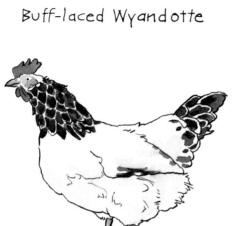

Light Sussex

Maran

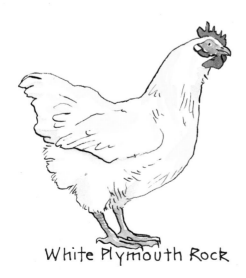

White Plymouth Rock

Silver Duckwing Old English Game

For Oscar Branson
K.W.
For Lynne
A.J.

First published 1993
by Walker Books Ltd
87 Vauxhall Walk
London SE11 5HJ

This book has been typeset in Calligraphic.

Printed and bound in Hong Kong by
South China Printing Co. (1988) Ltd

British Library Cataloguing in Publication Data
A catalogue record for this book is available
from the British Library.

ISBN 0-7445-2549-7

My Hen Is Dancing

Written by
Karen Wallace

Illustrated by
Anita Jeram

WALKER BOOKS
LONDON

My hen is dancing
in the farmyard.

She takes two
steps forward

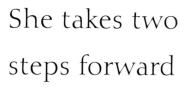

and one
step back.

She bends her neck and
pecks and scratches.

Her beak snaps shut.
She's found a worm.

A hen doesn't have teeth.
Food goes down into a pouch
in her body to be softened, then into
her gizzard, where it's ground up by
the bits of grit she swallows.

8

My hen is rolling
in her dustbath.

She likes the ground
when it's gritty and dry.

Dustbaths are good for cleaning
feathers and controlling fleas.

She cleans her feathers
with her beak and scratches
her ears with her toenails.

A hen also preens herself every day with oil.
It comes from where her tail feathers grow,
and she picks it up with her beak.

She stretches her wings
and sleeps in the sun.

My hen never struggles
if you hold her.

Her feathers are long
and smooth on her wings.

12

A hen can't fly far because her wings aren't strong, but she can flutter up and down from a perch.

Underneath she's soft
like a feather duster.
Her bones feel hard
like thin sticks inside her.

My hen lives in a henhouse
with five other hens.

There's fresh straw on the floor

and a row
of nestboxes
along the
back wall.

A cockerel lives there too. He has shiny tail feathers and a red coxcomb like a crown.

If my hen wanders,
he brings her home.

My hen lays big brown eggs.
When there are chicks
growing inside them,
she sits in her nestbox
and puffs up her feathers.

She pecks you if you try
to touch them.

Some kinds of hen lay brown eggs.
Some kinds of hen lay white eggs.
No kind of hen lays both.

A hen's chicks take three weeks to hatch.
She sits on the eggs, turning them every
day so that they stay warm all over.

While she is sitting on her eggs,
she is called a "broody" hen.

19

Her chicks are wet and

They creep underneath her

20

sticky when they hatch.

A newborn chick needs the warmth of its mother to survive.

where she's fluffy and warm.

My hen leads her chicks around the farmyard.

They learn to scratch and peck

and pull worms from the ground.

It takes about six months for a
chick to grow into a hen or a cockerel.

My hen knows when it's time to go to sleep.
As soon as it gets dark, she hops
into the henhouse.

She sleeps standing up.
Her long toes grip
the perch so she
doesn't fall.

Sleeping like this is called "roosting".

24

We close the henhouse door at night
to keep her safe from hungry foxes.

In the morning I open the door. The cockerel jumps out with my hen close behind him.

The cockerel crows and
she steps up beside him.

Hens eat all kinds of things, including corn,
crumbs, worms, insects, grass and vegetable scraps.

My hen is dancing
in the farmyard.

Black Leghorn

White Frizzle

Welsummer

Index

Silver-spangled Hamburg

White Transylvanian Naked-neck